Philippians — T
of Christi⸺

*This is a self-study course
designed to help you discover
for yourself, from the Bible,
some important basic truths about
living the Christian life.*

how to study the lesson

1. Try to find a quiet spot free from distractions and noise.

2. Read the entire Scripture lesson; read it several times to help you absorb its content.

3. Read each question carefully. Then look up the Scripture reference given after each question. Make sure you have found the correct Scripture passage. For example, sometimes you may find yourself looking up JOHN 1:1 instead of I JOHN 1:1.

4. Answer the question from the appropriate Bible passage. Write, in your own words, a phrase or sentence to answer the question. In questions that can be answered with a "yes" or "no" always give the reason for your answer . . . "Yes, because. . . ."

5. If possible, keep a dictionary handy in order to look up words you don't understand.

6. Pray for God's help. You *need* God's help in order to understand what you study in the Bible. Psalm 119:18 would be an appropriate verse for you to take to God in prayer.

7. *Class teachers using this course for group study will find some helpful suggestions on page 47.*

how to take the self-check tests

Each lesson is concluded with a test designed to help you evaluate what you have learned.

1. Review the lesson carefully in the light of the self-check test questions.

2. If there are any questions in the self-check test you cannot answer, perhaps you have written into your lesson the wrong answer from your Bible. Go over your work carefully to make sure you have filled in the blanks correctly.

3. When you think you are ready to take the self-check test, do so without looking up the answers.

4. Check your answers to the self-check test carefully with the answer key given on page 48.

5. If you have any questions wrong, your answer key will tell you where to find the correct answer in your lesson. Go back and locate the right answers. Learn by your mistakes!

apply what you have learned to your own life

In this connection, read carefully JAMES 1:22-25. It is only as you apply your lessons to your own life that you will really grow in grace and increase in the knowledge of God.

Introduction to Philippians

It was a moment fraught with far-reaching consequences when Paul heard the Macedonian call while at Troas (Acts 16:9). As a result, Europe heard the gospel for the first time.

Paul and his party dropped anchor at Neapolis, the port of Philippi on the other side of the mountain, and took the road to this city recognized by Philip of Macedon as a gateway to be strongly guarded. To remember this is to get new light on many expressions in this epistle.

Here, ten years before the date of this epistle, began friendships unbroken through the years, particularly with Timothy, a youth of exemplary ability and piety. It is the most personal of all Paul's church epistles.

It was written at Rome while Paul, a prisoner, was in Caesar's household (4:22) where the "whole praetorian guard" (A.S.V.) was found (1:13).

Outline

I. A Christian Salutation 1:1-11

II. A Prison Witness 1:12-30

III. The Mind of Christ 2:1-11

IV. The Outworkings of Salvation 2:12-30

V. Warnings Against Judaism 3:1-11

VI. The Christian Walk 3:12-21

VII. A Christian Exhortation 4:1-9

VIII. A Christian's Giving 4:10-23

A Christian's Salutation

1:1-11

1. How does Paul show his profound personal appropriation of God?

1:3 _____

2. How is his special attachment for the believers at Philippi indicated?

1:4 _____

_____

3. What did Paul experience as he made requests for them?

1:4 _____

It gives a minister peculiar joy to pray for some people. He can overlook many shortcomings when he can think of them as loyal, helpful, prayerful, and desiring only to advance the cause of Christ.

4. What was Paul's feeling of certainty about these believers?

1:6 _____

_____

In verse 6, the opening words are literally, "You can rely on this."

5. If we are now the sons of God, what can we know?

I John 3:2 _____

_____

6. What is Jesus Christ besides being the Author of our salvation?

Hebrews 12:1, 2 _____

7. Why is He able to save *unto* the uttermost (limit of time) even faulty believers?

Hebrews 7:25 _____

_____

8. Because of His intercession, what is assured to a truly born-again person?

Romans 8:33, 34 _____

9. In spite of our many shortcomings, what will He confirm (lit. "guarantee")?

I Corinthians 1:8 _____

10. What did our Lord say of all whom the Father had given Him through regeneration?

John 6:39 _____

_____

The merits of the atoning death of our Lord, plus His high priestly work, cannot fail a true child of God so that he will slip out of God's hands.

11. What did Jesus say about the security of the believer?

John 10:28, 29 _____

_____

12. While a child of God is expected to "work out" or manifest the implanted life, who works in him?

PHILIPPIANS 2:13 _____

13. What is the condition of the true Christian who falls by the wayside?

I CORINTHIANS 11:32; cf. PSALM 37:24 _____

_____   _____

A Christian is far more victorious in his life when he comes to believe in the *fidelity of God.* Dr. Hodge writes: "The apostle's confidence in the steadfastness and final perseverance of these believers was founded neither on their strength or their purpose to persevere, nor on any assumption that the principle of religion in their hearts was indestructible; but simply on the fidelity of God. If God has promised to give certain persons to His Son as His inheritance, to deliver them from sin and condemnation and to make them partakers of eternal life, it is certain He will not allow them to perish. This is plain enough; but how did the apostle know that those to whom he wrote were included in the number of those given to Christ and that the fidelity of God was pledged to their salvation? It was because they were called. Whom He calls, them He also justifies; and whom He justifies, them He also glorifies (ROMANS 8:30). The call intended is the effectual call of the Holy Spirit by which the soul is renewed and translated from the kingdom of darkness into the kingdom of light. The only evidence of election is therefore vocation, and the only evidence of vocation is holiness of heart and life, for we are called into the fellowship of His Son."

14. During Paul's days of imprisonment, for what group did he especially long?

1:8 _____

The word translated "bowels" is one that in Greek classics stood for the "nobler vitals." The translators conceived of the "bowels" as the seat of tender feelings. In our day we would refer to the "heart" instead. A modern translation gives: "I long after you in the very heart-root in Christ."

15. For what did Paul especially pray on their behalf?

1:9 _____

_____

16. In this prayer, what was Paul's concern about the genuineness of their Christian profession?

1:10 _____

_____

The Greek word for "sincere" is one that means "sun-tested." In making of porcelain ware, cracks needing wax filling were revealed by holding the pieces up to the sunlight. Hypocrisy is a wax that some people use to try to hide the imperfections of character.

17. What is the only way one can be filled with the acceptable fruits of righteousness?

1:11; cf. ROMANS 10:1-3 _____

_____

check-up time No. 1

You have just studied some important truths from Philippians 1:1-11. Review your study by rereading the questions and your written answers. If you wish, you may use the self-check test as an aid in reviewing your lesson. If you aren't sure of an answer, reread the Scripture portion given to see if you can find the answer. Then take this test to see how well you understand important truths you have studied.

In the right-hand margin write "True" or "False" after each of the following statements.

1. Timothy was with Paul when he was in Rome. _____

2. The church in Philippi had no organization. _____

3. Paul often remembered the saints of Philippi. _____

4. Paul often prayed for the saints of Philippi. _____

5. Even though God saves us, He leaves our Christian growth entirely in our hands. _____

6. Paul was released from prison before he wrote this letter to the Philippians. _____

7. Paul was always ready to defend his faith. _____

8. Paul prayed that the Philippians would grow in the knowledge of Christ. _____

9. The Philippians were to be concerned about their Christian character. _____

10. Christians can bring forth fruits of righteousness if they try hard enough. _____

Turn to page 48 and check your answers.

A Prison
Witness

1:12-30

1. What results may the endurance of persecution for Christ's sake have?

1:12 _____

2. What kind of uncontrollable blaze did Paul start by being a prison inmate in a Roman palace?

1:13, 14 _____

Most revivals have been kindled around some Christian in dead earnest. It is the prerogative of every Christian to be a center of kindling influence, rather than a mere recipient.

3. In what way did some men preach Christ?

1:15 _____

4. How did some preachers in Paul's day add to his burdens?

1:16 _____

The word for "contention" means "factiousness" or party work. They took advantage of Paul's situation to feather a nest for themselves.

5. Name one effective way to preach Christ.

1:17 _____

6. What was Paul's chief consolation?

1:18 _____

If the gospel is proclaimed so that some souls find salvation, it is better than no preaching at all. It is sometimes hard to rejoice in the good results of the work of men whose methods and motives are unquestionably bad, but we must look upon the truth as mighty enough to take care of itself.

7. Why did Paul believe the annoying efforts of workers who were playing politics would be turned to his good?

1:19 _____

8. Although Paul was now in obscurity, what did he still count upon?

1:20 _____

_____

9. Why may one who is in God's will have a holy indifference as to whether he is in the public eye or in the background?

1:21 _____

10. What is the sum and substance of a true Christian life anyway?

1:21 _____

11. What is a blessed possibility, even when the will of God keeps one in obscurity?

GALATIANS 4:19; cf. GALATIANS 2:20 _____

12. How is one changed into the image of Christ from one stage of glory to another?

II Corinthians 3:18 _____.

13. What takes place in the life of one wholly surrendered to the Lord Jesus?

Romans 12:2 _____

_____

14. Why did Paul have no fear of death, if that was God's will for him?

1:23; cf. 1:20 _____

_____

15. When a Christian departs by death, where is he going to be?

1:23 _____

16. With what one word does Paul describe death for the Christian?

1:23 _____

The Greek word for "depart" means "to be unloosed." It means to pull up the tent pegs and change encampment. Death to the Christian is not oblivion, but removal to the highlands.

17. What may have made Paul a bit homesick for the other land?

II Corinthians 12:2 _____

18. To be absent from the body meant what to Paul?

II Corinthians 5:8 _____

19. Although the *body* "sleeps" until the resurrection, what will the departed spirit do when Jesus comes?

I THESSALONIANS 4:13, 14 _____

20. How do we know that Paul did not have the idea he could communicate with his friends after death?

1:24 _____

21. What was the only way he could be of service to the Philippians for their spiritual advancement?

1:25 _____

22. What does Paul say about the believer's "conversation" (i.e. "citizenship")?

1:27a _____

_____

23. What was one thing Paul wanted to hear about them, even though not permitted to come to them?

1:27b _____

_____

24. Who is always at work to break up the unity of the church?

1:28 _____

25. What can those who believe in Christ expect?

1:29 _____

26. How did Paul know it is "given" to some people to suffer on behalf of Christ as well as to preach?

ACTS 9:15, 16 _____

_____

27. If his trials are the result of his witness for Christ, what can the suffering Christian do?

MATTHEW 5:12 _____

_____

28. What is especially acceptable to God?

I PETER 2:20, 21 _____

_____

check-up time No. 2

You have just studied some important truths from Philippians 1:12-30. Review your study by rereading the questions and your written answers. If you aren't sure of an answer, reread the Scripture portion given to see if you can find the answer. Then take the following test to see how well you understand important truths you have studied.

In the right-hand margin write "True" or "False" after each of the following statements.

1. Paul's imprisonment hindered the spread of the gospel. _____

2. Paul's influence had reached even into the palace in Rome. _____

3. Some men thought they could make Paul jealous by preaching the gospel. _____

4. Paul rejoiced that regardless of the motive, the gospel was being preached. _____

5. Paul felt that perhaps in the not too distant future he would lose his life. _____

6. Paul wanted to remain on earth, for he was afraid to die. _____

7. It would be better for the church if Paul became a martyr. _____

8. The Philippians would rejoice if Paul could pay them another visit. _____

9. The Philippians were to be agreed in matters of the gospel. _____

10. Those who believe on Christ will have a life of peace and quietness. _____

Turn to page 48 and check your answers.

The Mind of Christ

2:1-11

1. Name some of the greatest joys for a minister.

2:1, 2 _____

_____

2. What is the great antidote to disunity?

2:3 _____

One translation of the first phrase of verse 3 is: "Let nothing be done through partisanship and pomposity." This pair has been responsible for the ruin of many a good work.

3. If believers are to be "likeminded," what kind of minds are needed?

2:3 _____

4. In what way can believers be "likeminded"?

2:5 _____

One rendering of the words "esteem other better than themselves" is, "Let each give the other fellow the right of way."

5. How can we promote our best interests?

2:4 _____

6. What do our minds need?

ROMANS 12:2 _____

7. Whose work is it to show us the things of Christ?

JOHN 16:13, 14 _____

8. What did the Lord Jesus say we should do with our minds?

MATTHEW 22:37 _____

9. What are we told about the "carnal mind"?

ROMANS 8:7 _____

Insofar as we yield to Him, the mind of the Master will become the master of our minds.

As to lowliness of mind, the apostle now proceeds to give a wonderful illustration. He pictures the immensity of the stoop our Lord was willing to take for us—as if by putting such an amazing spectacle before us, it could not fail to blot out our exalted ideas of ourselves.

10. In what form was Christ before His incarnation?

2:6 _____

The literal translation of verse 6 is: "Who being that which is the very essence of God."

11. Christ was on what plane of equality compared with God the Father?

2:6 _____

A more literal translation of verse 6: He "did not deem his being on an equality with God a thing to be retained as a prize"—or something He might lose by taking the form of man.

12. What claim did Jesus make before men?

JOHN 5:18 _____

13. When He was about to return to heaven, what did Jesus pray?

JOHN 17:5 _____

_____

14. What was Christ's place before He came to earth?

HEBREWS 1:2, 3 _____

_____

15. Of whom is Christ the image?

COLOSSIANS 1:15 _____

16. What was Christ's part in creation?

COLOSSIANS 1:16 _____

_____

17. State what the incarnation meant to Christ.

2:7 _____

_____

The original here means that He "emptied Himself"—not of His deity, but that He divested Himself of His glory and restrained Himself in the use of His divine powers so that He could pass among men as a servant. The glory of God was still in Him, manifested often in beneficent deeds and words of wisdom (JOHN 1:14), and a few glimpses of His unapproachable glory were given (MATTHEW 17:2); yet He used His miraculous powers, not for self-defense, but only for the help of others. He was still the same divine Person of the God-head, although instead of the form of deity, for a time He condescended to take the form of a bondservant.

18. What did Jesus give up for our sakes?

II Corinthians 8:9 _____

_____

19. How was His heavenly origin manifested even when He was a child?

Luke 2:47 _____

_____

The Second Person of the Trinity made Himself such a perfect Servant that His Father said: "Behold my servant, in whom my soul delighteth." After having from eternal ages known only to command, He gave Himself up only to obey. What a pattern of lowliness of mind for us!

20. How far down was the infinite Son willing to go for us?

2:8 _____

_____

21. In what way did He voluntarily make Himself weak?

Matthew 27:40, 42 _____

_____

Here was His weakness—voluntary weakness: He refused to use His own inherent powers to save Himself and come down from the cross. He gave in to the death of the cross, submitted to the worst possible indignities as though He were the weakest of men—*because* that emptied condition was the necessary step in providing redemption for lost sinners.

22. How is our strength sometimes made perfect?

II Corinthians 12:9 _____

23. By what stupendous act did God exalt Christ after He had reached the bottom rung of the ladder?

2:9; cf. ROMANS 1:4 _____

24. Where did Stephen see the Lord Jesus?

ACTS 7:55 _____

25. Who is now the one Mediator between God and men?

I TIMOTHY 2:5 _____

26. What is the name that is above every name?

2:9, 10 _____

check-up time No. 3

You have just studied some important truths from Philippians 2:1-11. Review your study by rereading the questions and your written answers. If you aren't sure of an answer, reread the Scripture portion given to see if you can find the answer. Then take this test to see how well you understand important truths you have studied.

In the right-hand margin write "True" or "False" after each of the following statements.

1. If the Philippians were of the same mind, Paul would be happy. _____

2. The Philippians were to have great pride in their accomplishments. _____

3. Christians are to have respect for one another. _____

4. Christians are to have the mind of Christ. _____

5. Christians should have a concern over the welfare of others. _____

6. Christ is a little lower than God the Father in the Trinity. _____

7. Christ came to this earth as a highly honored King. _____

8. Even though Jesus was the Son of God, He was also man. _____

9. There will come a time when every knee will bow to Jesus Christ. _____

10. The name of Jesus is supreme so far as God is concerned. _____

Turn to page 48 and check your answers.

The Outworkings of Salvation

2:12-30

1. Whether saved or unsaved, how many are going to be compelled to acknowledge the deity of Christ?

2:10, 11 _____

_____

2. What same claim is made for Jesus as for Jehovah in the Old Testament?

ISAIAH 45:23; cf. ROMANS 14:10, 11 _____

_____

3. While some will enjoy everlasting life, what will others awake to find?

DANIEL 12:2 _____

4. How would Paul teach those at Philippi to be independent of him?

2:12 _____

Paul is saying: "You're on your own—be watchful. Fully sense your responsibility." There is no suggestion here of salvation by works.

5. So that no one would trust in his own good works, what did Paul add?

2:13 _____

_____

6. If we do any good works as Christians, what must we all admit?

ISAIAH 26:12 _____

7. How is that which is well pleasing to God produced in us?

HEBREWS 13:20, 21 _____

_____

8. To what must we give the credit for everything that pertains to life and godliness?

II PETER 1:3 _____

The "fear and trembling" of PHILIPPIANS 2:12 is not tormenting misgivings about salvation (see I JOHN 4:18). It is a wakeful conscience as one who lives in the presence of God.

9. What two things seriously hurt the cause of Christ?

2:14 _____

In verse 14 the word for "murmurings" means "grouchiness."

10. State our primary business as representatives of the Light of the world.

2:15 _____

One rendering of verse 15 is, "Shine like stars in a dark world."

11. Although stars are faulty lights (JOB 25:5), what service can they render?

JEREMIAH 31:35 _____

12. What is the best lamp for us to hold forth to lighten the path of others?

2:16; cf. Psalm 119:105 _____

13. Who can be certain in the day of the Lord's coming, that he has not labored in vain?

2:16 _____

14. As Paul looked forward to the future recognition of his converts at the judgment seat, what did he know he could count upon?

I Thessalonians 2:19, 20 _____

_____

15. What is one way to assure oneself of great joy in that day?

2:15; cf. Daniel 12:3 _____

_____

Dr. Campbell Morgan points out that the word for "lights" in Philippians 2:15 occurs in only one other place—Revelation 21:11, referring to the light of the Holy City: "Her light was like unto a stone most precious." The reference is not to a light the city itself diffused, but a light she received. "The light thereof is the Lamb, and the nations shall walk amidst the light thereof" (see Revelation 21:23, 24). Thus the Lamb is to be in final glory, all its light. Let us not forget that this is what God's children are called to be to a lost world today—lights for Him in a dark world.

16. What was Paul's opinion of Timothy?

2:20 _____

_____

17. In contrast, what was Paul's opinion of some other Christian workers?

2:21 _____

_____

18. Who was Paul sending as a messenger to Philippi?

2:25 _____

19. Why had not Epaphroditus left earlier?

2:26, 27 _____

20. How were the Philippians to receive him?

2:29 _____

_____

21. What was Paul's hope even in prison?

2:24 _____

_____

check-up time No. 4

You have just studied some important truths from Philippians 2:12-30. Review your study by rereading the questions and your written answers. If you aren't sure of an answer, reread the Scripture portion given to see if you can find the answer. Then take this test to see how well you understand important truths you have studied.

In the right-hand margin write "True" or "False" after each of the following statements.

1. It is God who works in the Christian and helps him to please God. _____

2. Christians are to serve without complaining. _____

3. Christians really make very little impact upon the world. _____

4. Paul desired to keep Timothy with him at all times. _____

5. There are some who are more concerned about their own things than the things of Christ. _____

6. Paul hoped to visit Philippi himself in the future. _____

7. Paul probably sent this letter with Epaphroditus. _____

8. Epaphroditus was sick while in Rome. _____

9. The Philippians were to receive Epaphroditus with joy. _____

10. Epaphroditus was willing to give his life for the cause of the gospel. _____

Turn to page 48 and check your answers.

Warnings Against Judaism

3:1-11

1. Although Paul was in prison, how did he boldly counsel Christians?

3:1 _____

2. What is the secret of this spring of eternal joy in the heart?

3:3 _____

3. Why is it fitting that a Christian should always rejoice?

PSALM 5:11 _____

4. What is a two-word Christian command?

I THESSALONIANS 5:16 _____

5. List the three warnings that Paul gave.

3:2 _____

In the East dogs are rarely individually owned. They roam in packs as unclean scavengers. In some Bible passages they are the symbol of religious emissaries (ISAIAH 56:10; II PETER 2:22, etc.). The word for "concision" used here means "body mutilators," a derisive term used of Judaizers who tried to hinge salvation on the obsolete rite of circumcision.

27

6. What is the spiritual circumcision that is essential?

3:3; cf. ROMANS 2:28, 29 _____

7. In his religious sincerity and zeal, what had Paul done?

3:6 _____

8. How far had he gone in his ceremonial religiousness?

3:6 _____

9. Even though zeal is a divine quality, what can sometimes happen ?

ROMANS 10:2 _____

10. What did Paul have to charge off as a total loss in the end?

3:7 _____

11. What did Paul gain in place of self-centered religiousness?

3:8 _____

12. How did he come to feel about the comparative value of his old life of Judaism?

3:8 _____

13. Where does the gospel of works lead us?

PROVERBS 14:12 _____

14. For what must one exchange self-righteousness before he can find peace with God?

3:9 _____

15. Even though one's own way may be a fairly good way, what must he have to be acceptable to God?

ISAIAH 53:5, 6 _____

_____

16. Through faith, where did Paul finally find himself?

3:9 _____

17. Through union with Christ, what new living power did Paul come to know?

3:10 _____

18. In order to be true to Christ, what did he find he must share?

3:10 _____

19. What did Christ's resurrection prove Him to be?

ROMANS 1:4 _____

20. How much power is the risen Christ able to release?

MATTHEW 28:18 _____

21. What is the power that is now available to believers?

EPHESIANS 1:19, 20 _____

_____

22. Describe the kind of life the Christian should enjoy.

JOHN 10:10b _____

_____

23. If we expect to be channels of this power, what must we be willing to be made?

3:10 _____

24. If we have met these conditions, of what may we be positively assured?

3:11 _____

Verse 11 literally refers to "the out-resurrection from among the dead." All the dead are not to be raised at the same time. When our Lord comes for His Church, His saints will be called "out from among" the dead (I THESSALONIANS 4:13-16).

25. What two great resurrections are distinguished?

JOHN 5:28, 29 _____

_____

26. At least how long will it be after the saints are resurrected, before the bodies of the unsaved will be raised?

REVELATION 20:4-6 _____

_____

check-up time No. 5

You have just studied some important truths from
Philippians 3:1-11. Review your study by rereading
the questions and your written answers. If you aren't
sure of an answer, reread the Scripture portion given
to see if you can find the answer. Then take this
test to see how well you understand important truths
you have studied.

In the right-hand margin write "True" or "False"
after each of the following statements.

1. It grieved Paul to have to write the same things
again to the Philippians.

2. Paul warned the Philippians against enemies that
would divide the church.

3. A Christian should have no confidence in the flesh
when it comes to pleasing God.

4. Paul could trace his ancestry back to the tribe of
Levi.

5. As far as Paul's religious faith was concerned, he
was a Pharisee.

6. Paul counted his religious heritage as something to
be proud of.

7. Paul would give up all things for the knowledge of
Christ.

8. Paul was saved by his righteousness as a Pharisee
who kept the law.

9. Paul desired to know the power of Christ's resurrection in his own life.

10. Paul did not look forward to the suffering that
goes with the Christian life.

Turn to page 48 and check your answers.

The Christian Walk

3:12-21

1. By whom was Paul apprehended for Christian service?

3:12 _____

2. How did he know he had already been apprehended?

1:6 _____

_____

3. Having the seal of salvation, how long did he expect it to hold him?

EPHESIANS 1:13, 14 _____

_____

4. Although Paul counted himself far from "perfect," when did he know he would be perfect?

I JOHN 3:2 _____

Pity the man who thinks he has attained the place where nothing is to be added, and where he is now wholly sanctified. He is most blessed who, as he mounts ever higher, sees perfection afar off—in Christ.

5. With the resurrection power of Christ in him, and the hope of bodily resurrection before him, what was Paul's life motive?

3:14 _____

Note that Paul's ground of confidence was not in any elevation he had attained, but in the fact that Christ had apprehended him. He would fully realize all that His Lord had for him in His plan, and would take fast hold of the things for which Christ had taken fast hold of him.

6. With this assurance in Christ, what were some of the things Paul could now conveniently "forget"?

3:13; cf. VERSES 4-6 _____

7. When once "in Chirst," what is a good motto for every Christian?

PROVERBS 4:25 _____

_____

8. What is the "high calling" toward which Christians press?

TITUS 2:13; II TIMOTHY 4:8; THESSALONIANS 4:17 _____

_____

Some authorities give verse 14 as "the prize of the calling up to God on high." This is the rapture of the Church.

9. How is our spiritual maturity cared for?

3:14 _____

10. In what class did Paul put those who did not walk (live) as he walked (lived)?

3:18 _____

11. Where is the Christian's citizenship?

3:20 _____

Bishop Moule says the word rendered "conversation" here means "city home or commonwealth." Here is the patriotism of the soul.

12. Who is coming down some day from the home city?

3:20 _____

13. What part of the believer will be affected at Christ's coming?

3:21 _____

14. How will the bodies of all believers be transformed?

3:21 _____

The rendering "vile body" is unfortunate. Some give, "the body of our humiliation," or the body that belongs to our low estate here. It is a frail tenement in which the Spirit sojourns for this life. It returns to dust (ECCLESIASTES 12:7). Nevertheless as the companion of our spirit, and the temple of the Holy Spirit during life, the body is reserved for a higher destiny than remaining dust.

check-up time No. 6

You have just studied some important truths from Philippians 3:12-21. Review your study by rereading the questions and your written answers. If you aren't sure of an answer, reread the Scripture portion given to see if you can find the answer. Then take this test to see how well you understand important truths you have studied.

In the right-hand margin write "True" or "False" after each of the following statements.

1. Paul felt that by this time he had attained to the fullness of the Christian life. _____

2. Paul wished to push on toward his goal and forget things of the past. _____

3. God will reveal the truth to us. _____

4. Christians should be agreed in the things of the Christian life. _____

5. Paul said that other believers should follow him as an example of the Christian life. _____

6. Many of those that try to influence Christians in religious errors are enemies of Christ. _____

7. The enemies of Christ are interested in satisfying the lusts of the flesh. _____

8. The enemies of Christ seek after heavenly things. _____

9. The Christian's real citizenship (conversation) is on this earth. _____

10. The power of Christ is even able to change our present body into a glorified body. _____

Turn to page 48 and check your answers.

A Christian's Exhortation

4:1-9

Having pointed out the dignity of Christian citizenship and exalted conduct befitting those having such privileges, the apostle now exhorts to steadfastness in support of those loyal to Christ.

1. How can believers be enabled to "stand fast in the Lord"?

4:1; PSALM 27:14 _____

_____

2. To what may such steadfast believers be compared?

PSALM 125:1 _____

3. What was Paul's evaluation of Euodias and Syntyche?

4:3 _____

4. What appears to have occurred between the two women that distressed Paul?

4:2 _____

5. While the names of many obscure missionary workers may not be known on earth, where are they registered?

4:3 _____

36

6. What keynote of the epistle is again sounded here?

4:4 _____

7. State one of Paul's rules for living.

4:4 _____

_____

8. What prayer does many a Christian need to pray?

Psalm 51:12 _____

_____

9. What does it sometimes take to get back the power to radiate Christian joy?

Psalm 32:4, 5 _____

10. Name one certain mark of a God-controlled life.

4:5 _____

In verse 5 the word for "moderation" means "considerateness" or as one translates it, "sweet reasonableness."

11. What truth helps to give one a vivid sense of the need of this well-balanced life?

4:5 _____

12. In how many matters should a Christian manifest a spirit of "anxious care"?

4:6 _____

13. What is the sure antidote for the spirit of anxiety?

4:6 _____

14. For what will anxiety then be exchanged?

4:7 _____

15. What element needs to be well mixed with prayer (petition) and supplication (pleading of promises)?

4:6 _____

16. What two departments of the Christian life may be kept (lit. "garrisoned") by God's perfect peace?

4:7 _____

The "heart" represents the seat of the affections; the "mind," the seat of the thought life.

17. Though perplexities may sometimes wall us around, what will keep them from roofing us over?

PSALM 55:22 _____

18. How should the peace of God affect us?

COLOSSIANS 3:15 _____

19. Why is there no need to let our minds be in a turmoil?

JOHN 14:27 _____

_____

20. In whom must the virtues here mentioned be rooted?

4:8; cf. VERSE 4 _____

_____

21. What is one necessary step toward realizing these virtues in character?

4:8 _____

Those who enthrone Christ in the sanctuary of the mind will stop gravitating and will reach out for the characteristics seen in His life. Every thought of heavenly things contributes to the making of character.

22. What did Paul say about following his example?

4:9 _____

23. To what extent did he want others to be followers of him?

I CORINTHIANS 11:1; I THESSALONIANS 1:6 _____

Some preach so well in the pulpit, it is a tragedy they ever go out of it. They live so poorly, it is unfortunate that they ever enter it.

24. If others followed Paul's example, what would they experience?

4:9 _____

check-up time No. 7

You have just studied some important truths from Philippians 4:1-9. Review your study by rereading the questions and your written answers. If you aren't sure of an answer, reread the Scripture portion given to see if you can find the answer. Then take this test to see how well you understand important truths you have studied.

In the right-hand margin write "True" or "False" after each of the following statements.

1. Paul urged the Philippians to stand fast in the Lord. ＿＿＿＿＿

2. The two women leaders in the Philippian church were very friendly to each other. ＿＿＿＿＿

3. Paul expected the other Christians to help the two women solve their problems. ＿＿＿＿＿

4. Those that labor in the gospel have their names in the book of life. ＿＿＿＿＿

5. A Christian is to be moderate (i.e. considerate) in all things. ＿＿＿＿＿

6. Paul instructed the Christians that the Lord's second coming was yet a great way off. ＿＿＿＿＿

7. Christians are to be greatly concerned about their circumstances. ＿＿＿＿＿

8. Christians are to be people of prayer. ＿＿＿＿＿

9. The peace of God can be fully understood by the Christian. ＿＿＿＿＿

10. Paul insisted that the Philippians follow in the faith as he had instructed them. ＿＿＿＿＿

Turn to page 48 and check your answers.

A Christian's Giving

4:10-23

1. How was Paul able to find contentment in any circumstances?

4:11 _____

2. Why was Paul now rejoicing over the Philippians?

4:10 _____

_____

3. Why had not the Philippian church sent a gift earlier?

4:10 _____

4. How did Paul respond to the Philippian's gift?

4:10 _____

5. What is sufficient to make anyone contented even in the poorest of earthly circumstances?

HEBREWS 13:5 _____

6. How can we effectively use the little word "can"?

4:13 _____

7. List the six experiences the apostle Paul had gone through during his ministry.

4:12 _____

_____

_____

8. Why did Jesus say that we must abide in Him?

JOHN 15:5 (latter part) _____

9. What is the cause of most of our failures?

II CORINTHIANS 3:4, 5 _____

_____

10. List the three great "shalls" of this chapter.

4:7 _____

_____

4:9 _____

4:19 _____

_____

11. What did Paul have to say about the other Macedonian churches?

4:15 _____

_____

12. Even though Paul appreciated the gift, what did he desire more than the gift?

4:17 _____

_____

13. Who had been sent with the gift?

4:18 _____

14. How would God look upon this gift to Paul?

4:18 _____

_____

15. Since God does not supply our whims, what does He supply?

4:19 _____

16. Who is the best judge of our real needs?

MATTHEW 6:25-32 _____

17. What does God never withhold?

PSALM 84:11 _____

18. What does God sometimes have to do while He supplies our true needs?

DEUTERONOMY 8:3, 4 _____

19. What is one condition of God's favor that Christians sometimes overlook?

PROVERBS 3:9, 10 _____

20. Why does God keep some people in straightened circumstances?

PROVERBS 3:9, 10 _____

_____

21. What keeps God from pouring out blessings upon some?

MALACHI 3:10 _____

_____

22. What does the Father long to do for us all?

II Corinthians 9:8 _____

_____

We like to plan our own method of relief and instruct Him as to what He should send us. He usually disregards our plans in order to give us something far better. Our supply may come from a most unexpected source, but when it comes, we know that none but a loving Father could have sent it.

23. How is it possible for God to pour out His blessings upon us?

4:19 _____

_____

24. How do we know that Paul must have won some of the members of the palace household to Christ?

4:22 _____

_____

check-up time No. 8

You have just studied some important truths from Philippians 4:10-23. Review your study by rereading the questions and your written answers. If you aren't sure of an answer, reread the Scripture portion given to see if you can find the answer. Then take this test to see how well you understand the important truths you have studied.

In the right-hand margin write "True" or "False" after each of the following statements.

1. Paul could rejoice even though he was in prison. _____

2. The Philippians were not able to help Paul while he was in prison. _____

3. Paul always spoke out when he needed things other Christians could supply. _____

4. Paul found it hard to be content while confined to prison. _____

5. There were times when the apostle Paul was not in need. _____

6. The power of Christ enables Christians to accomplish many things. _____

7. The churches in Macedonia helped in the support of the apostle Paul. _____

8. A Christian's giving is one mark of Christian faithfulness. _____

9. God will supply all the needs of a Christian. _____

10. There were no Christians in Caesar's household. _____

Turn to page 48 and check your answers.

Suggestions for class use

1. The class teacher may wish to tear this page from each workbook as the answer key is on the reverse side.

2. The teacher should study the lesson first, filling in the blanks in the workbook. He should be prepared to give help to the class on some of the harder places in the lesson. He should also take the self-check tests himself, check his answers with the answer key and look up any question answered incorrectly.

3. Class sessions can be supplemented by the teacher's giving a talk or leading a discussion on the subject to be studied. The class could then fill in the workbook together as a group, in teams, or individually. If so desired by the teacher, however, this could be done at home. The self-check tests can be done as homework by the class.

4. The self-check tests can be corrected at the beginning of each class session. A brief discussion of the answers can serve as review for the previous lesson.

5. The teacher should motivate and encourage his students. Some public recognition might well be given to class members who successfully complete this course.

Moody Press, a ministry of the Moody Bible Institute, is designed for education, evangelization and edification. If we may assist you in knowing more about Christ and the Christian life, please write us without obligation to: Moody Press, c/o MLM, Chicago, Illinois 60610.

answer key
to self-check tests

Be sure to look up any questions you answered incorrectly.

Q gives the number of the test *question*.

A gives the correct *answer*.

R *refers* you to the Scripture verse in Philippians where the correct answer is to be found.

Mark with an "x" your wrong answers, if any.

TEST 1			TEST 2			TEST 3			TEST 4		
Q	A	R	Q	A	R	Q	A	R	Q	A	R
1	T	1:1	1	F	1:12	1	T	2:2	1	T	2:13
2	F	1:1	2	T	1:13	2	F	2:3	2	T	2:14
3	T	1:3	3	T	1:15	3	T	2:3	3	F	2:15
4	T	1:4	4	T	1:18	4	T	2:5	4	F	2:19
5	F	1:6	5	T	1:20	5	T	2:4	5	T	2:21
6	F	1:7	6	F	1:23	6	F	2:6	6	T	2:24
7	T	1:7	7	F	1:24	7	F	2:7	7	T	2:25
8	T	1:9	8	T	1:26	8	T	2:8	8	T	2:27
9	T	1:10	9	T	1:27	9	T	2:10	9	T	2:29
10	F	1:11	10	F	1:29	10	T	2:9	10	T	2:30

TEST 5			TEST 6			TEST 7			TEST 8		
Q	A	R	Q	A	R	Q	A	R	Q	A	R
1	F	3:1	1	F	3:12	1	T	4:1	1	T	4:10
2	T	3:2	2	T	3:13	2	F	4:2	2	F	4:10
3	T	3:3	3	T	3:15	3	T	4:3	3	F	4:11
4	F	3:5	4	T	3:16	4	T	4:3	4	F	4:11
5	T	3:5	5	T	3:17	5	T	4:5	5	T	4:12
6	F	3:7	6	T	3:18	6	F	4:5	6	T	4:13
7	T	3:8	7	T	3:19	7	F	4:6	7	F	4:15
8	F	3:9	8	F	3:19	8	T	4:6	8	T	4:17
9	T	3:10	9	F	3:20	9	F	4:7	9	T	4:19
10	F	3:10	10	T	3:21	10	T	4:9	10	F	4:22

How well
did
you do?

0-1 wrong answers on any one test—excellent work

2-3 wrong answers on any one test—review these items carefully

4 or more wrong answers—restudy the lesson before going on to the next one